The Olympics

Paul Shipton

Level 3

Series Editors: Andy Hopkins and Jocelyn Potter

Pearson Education Limited
Edinburgh Gate, Harlow,
Essex CM20 2JE, England
and Associated Companies throughout the world.

ISBN: 978-1-4082-6407-2

This edition first published by Pearson Education Ltd 2012

1 3 5 7 9 10 8 6 4 2

Illustrations by Oxford Designers and Illustrators, Redpaper Design

The moral right of the author has been asserted in accordance with
the Copyright Designs and Patents Act 1988
Set in 11/13pt A. Garamond
Printed in China (SWTC/01)
Produced for the Publishers by Red Paper Design

Published by Pearson Education Ltd in association with Penguin Books Ltd,
both companies being subsidiaries of Pearson Plc

Acknowledgements

The publisher would like to thank the following for their kind permission
to reproduce their photographs:

Alamy Images: INTERFOTO 5, The Art Gallery Collection 3; **Corbis:** Bettmann 52, Leo Mason 46,
Sampics ivtl; **Fotolia.com:** Yannik Labbe 56tl, Roberto Romanin 56cr; **Getty Images:** 6, 14, AFP 44, AFP
/ Leon Neal iv (bobsleigh), AFP / Mladen Antonov 38, AFP / Pascal Pavani 55, Allsport / Simon Bruty
51, Allsport / Tony Duffy 27, Lars Baron 28, Al Bello iv (skiing), Bongarts / Lars Baron 15, Bongarts /
Lutz Bongarts 36, Mark Dadswell iv (discus), Tony Duffy 29, Julian Finney ivtr, Stu Forster iv (hurdles),
Harry How ivbr, Hulton Archive 9, Hulton Archive / Keystone 26, Jed Jacobsohn 43, NBAE / Andrew
D. Bernstein 13, Popperfoto 25, Clive Rose iv (fencing), Cameron Spencer 1, Sports Illustrated / Manny
Millan 47, Sports Illustrated / Simon Bruty ivbc; **Photolibrary.com:** Tao Images 18-19; **Press Association
Images:** AP Photo / Andy Wong 17, AP Photo / Eric Gay ivbl, AP Photo / Thomas Kienzle 33, DPA 35,
PA Archive / Gareth Copley 16; **Rex Features:** Giuliano Bevilacqua iv (ice hockey), Jussi Nukari ivtc,
Sipa Press 39; **www.imagesource.com:** 56-57

Every effort has been made to trace the copyright holders and we apologise in advance for
any unintentional omissions. We would be pleased to insert the appropriate acknowledgement
in any subsequent edition of this publication.

For a complete list of the titles in the Penguin Active Reading series please go to www.penguinreaders.com.
Alternatively, write to your local Pearson Longman office or to: Penguin Readers Marketing Department,
Pearson Education, Edinburgh Gate, Harlow, Essex CM20 2JE, England.

Contents

1.1 What's the book about?

Look at the pictures below and talk to another student.

1 Which of these sports have you tried?

2 Which would you like to try? Why (not)?

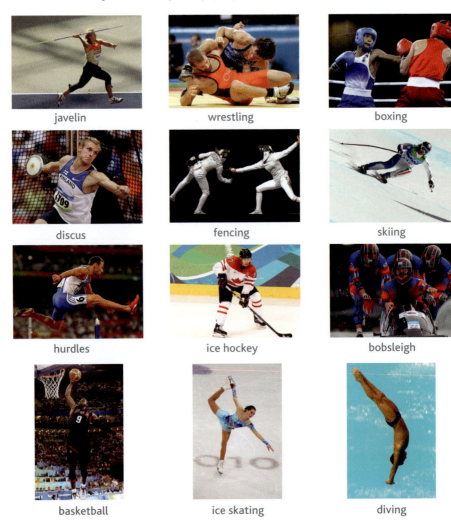

javelin

wrestling

boxing

discus

fencing

skiing

hurdles

ice hockey

bobsleigh

basketball

ice skating

diving

1.2 What comes first?

The Olympic Games were first held in Greece thousands of years ago. How do you think they were different from the modern Olympics? How do you think they were the same? Make two lists in your notebook.

CHAPTER 1

The First Olympic Games

Only the best of the best can win at the Olympics. This fact was as true thousands of years ago as it is in the modern Olympics.

Every four years the eyes of the world turn towards the biggest, most important **competition** in all of sport – the Olympic Games. The Games bring together thousands of the best **athletes** in the world – the fastest, the strongest, the most skilful in their sports. These men and women come from every corner of the world. Every one of them has **trained** hard, and for most of them the Games are the high point of their lives as sportspeople. They are all looking for the same thing – an Olympic gold **medal**.

Brazilian gold medalists at the Beijing Games in 2008.

Only the best of the best can win at the Olympics. This fact was as true thousands of years ago as it is in the modern Olympics. But in other ways, the early Olympic Games in Greece were quite different from the Games of today.

---

competition /ˌkɒmpəˈtɪʃən/ (n) an event in which people try to be more successful than other people. They **compete** in the event against other **competitors**.
athlete /ˈæθliːt/ (n) a sportsman or woman
train /treɪn/ (v) to prepare for a sport with practice and exercise; to help someone do this. A **trainer** trains athletes.
medal /ˈmedl/ (n) a round piece of metal given to winners in a competition. A winner of a medal for sport is a **medallist**.

The Birth of the Olympic Games

Nobody knows the date exactly, but the Olympic Games started more than 2,700 years ago, in Greece. Like the modern Games, they were held every four years, but they were always in the same place – Olympia, in southwest Greece. This was an important place in Greek religion, and the Games were more than just a sports competition to the Greeks.

At that time, Greece was not a single country; it was a number of different cities and states, each with its own government. These states were often at war, but they had an agreement: wars had to stop during the time of the Olympic Games. Because of this, athletes from all over Greece could travel to Olympia and compete at the Games without danger.

In the very early years, there was only one competition at the Games in Olympia – a race on foot. This race was short – less than 200 metres long – and twenty athletes could run at the same time. These athletes never wore shoes. In fact, in most sports at the Greek Olympic Games athletes did not wear any clothes.

At the start, the Olympic Games were not open to all athletes. Competitors had to be Greek-speakers and they had to be male. Married women could not even go to *watch* the games in Olympia. By law, the **organisers** of the Games could kill women who broke these rules. There was a story about a mother who wanted to watch her son in the Games. She dressed as a male trainer and went to the **stadium**. When her son won, the mother shouted happily. Immediately, her secret was discovered. Because she came from a famous sporting family, she did not face the worst punishment, of death. But after she was sent home, there was a new rule at the Olympics. Now trainers too wore no clothes!

As time passed, new sports were introduced to the Games.

● Running

Longer races were added. In one of them, the runners had to run from one end of the **track** to the other, turn around and run back again. In another race ('the long one') athletes had to run twenty-four times around the track (almost 5,000 metres). The Greeks did not keep records of the fastest times. Runners had to reach the end before the other competitors. Probably the most unusual foot race was introduced about 2,500 years ago. Athletes had to run carrying a soldier's heavy equipment with them.

---

organiser /ˈɔːgənaɪzə/ (n) someone who plans something. When it is **organised**, it is ready.
stadium /ˈsteɪdiəm/ (n) a large area for playing sports, with seats around it
track /træk/ (n) the part of a stadium where athletes run

● Horse races

In another area near the stadium, there were horse races. Nobody sat on the backs of the horses; drivers in open vehicles with wheels were pulled by teams of horses. There were different races – the longest was about 13 kilometres – with different numbers of horses. The vehicles were small and light with just two wheels. They were built to be fast. There were sometimes crashes during races and drivers often fell out.

These horse races were different from other sports at the Olympic Games in important ways. First, the drivers could wear clothes. Also, the driver of the fastest team was not thought to be the winner. The *owner* of the horses was the winner. This was the only way for a woman to compete at the Games, as the owner of horses in a race.

A horse race at the early Olympics in Greece

● Fighting sports

There were three different fighting sports in the early Olympic Games.

Boxing

In the Olympics today, boxers fight others of about the same weight, so lighter men can win medals. In the early Greek Olympic Games, successful boxers were usually big, strong men. They were given no rests in the middle of a fight. They fought until there was a winner. Some fights lasted all day!

Wrestling

Wrestling was a popular sport in Greece and the rules were similar to the rules of the sport today. A wrestler lost when his shoulders or back touched the ground three times. There were some differences from the modern sport. One wrestler, for example, was not able to throw the other fighter, but he still won. He did this by breaking the other man's fingers!

'Pankration'

This sport was probably even more dangerous than boxing or wrestling. The rules were simple: there were almost no rules! Fighters could hit, kick, wrestle, and break fingers and arms. It was almost like a street fight, but fighters could not bite or attack the eyes. If they did, a judge hit them with a long stick in the middle of the fight. Sometimes athletes even died in *pankration* fights. When this happened, the dead man was named the winner!

> ### Olympic Greats – Milo of Croton
>
> Probably the most famous athlete in Greece was a wrestler called Milo of Croton. He won at the Games six times, more than 2,500 years ago. He was a big, strong man. It was said that he ate 9 kilos of meat and 9 kilos of bread every day. Milo's name was known all around Greece. Once, the soldiers of Croton were preparing to fight the soldiers of another city-state. There were many more enemy soldiers, but then Milo arrived and filled the enemy with fear.

● The pentathlon

The winner of this competition was probably the best general athlete. He had to be big and strong for wrestling, but he had to be fast for running too. There was also a jump event in the **pentathlon**. People have called this the long jump, but it was very different from the modern long jump. Athletes could hold metal weights in their hands. These helped them to jump farther. The other two **events** in the pentathlon were throwing sports – the discus and the javelin.

The Last Days

The Games were still popular when the Romans took Greece. The Romans loved sports too. They were happy for the Games to continue. One year Nero – the most important man in all of Rome – decided to compete in the Olympics. He chose the horse race for drivers with ten horses. Nero was not the most skilful driver: he fell to the ground and did not even finish the race. Of course, that did not matter: the judges named him the winner.

The Olympics finally ended in the year 393. By that time, the world was changing and the Games were not so important. There were no more Olympic Games for 1500 years …

---

pentathlon /penˈtæθlən/ (n) a sports competition with five different sports. Competitors must do all of them.
event /ɪˈvent/ (n) one of the races or competitions that are part of a large sports competition

CHAPTER 2

The Birth of the Modern Olympics

*For Coubertin, sport was more than just fun or exercise; it was almost a religion.
In his words, man could 'know himself' through sport.*

Sport was one of the most important things in the world for Pierre de Coubertin (1863-1937). This rich man lived in Paris in the late 1800s. For Coubertin, sport was more than just fun or exercise; it was almost a religion. In his words, man could 'know himself' through sport. (*Man*, not *woman*. Like many people at that time, Coubertin did not really believe in the idea of sport for women.)

Pierre de Coubertin

Coubertin wanted to start a sports competition for athletes from many different countries. The first Olympic stadium at Olympia was discovered earlier in the 1800s and people learned again about the old Olympic Games. To Coubertin, the idea of those first Games seemed perfect for his international competition. He travelled to many countries and explained his dream: he wanted to bring back the Olympic Games.

Coubertin's Rules

At first, Coubertin did not find much interest in his idea. But at an international meeting in Paris in 1894, he presented his plan to people from different countries. He explained five main rules for the modern Olympics:

- The Olympics are held every four years.
- Each Olympic Games is held in a different country.
- There must be some modern sports in the Games.
- No children can compete.
- The winners must not receive any money.

At this meeting, he tried to give the idea of the Games in just three words: *Citius, Altius, Fortius.* In English, these Latin words mean 'Faster, Higher, Stronger.' The Games should be a stage for the best in all sports.

The time for Coubertin's idea was right. Twelve countries agreed to compete at a new Olympic Games in 1896. Because the first Olympics were in Greece, the first modern Olympics were planned for Greece too.

The First Modern Games

The Games were held in Athens in June 1896. Two hundred and forty-five athletes – all men! – from fourteen countries came to compete. One hundred and sixty-four of the competitors were from Greece; the rest of the athletes came from other European countries or from the United States. Some competitors did not even know about the Games before they went to Greece: Irish tennis player John Boland was only there on holiday. He won two medals at the Games!

Then and Now

In today's Olympics, swimming events take place in the best swimming pools. It was very different at the first modern Olympic Games in Athens. The swimmers competed in the cold waters of the Mediterranean Sea.

For the 1,200 metres race, three small boats took the swimmers out to sea. At the sound of a gun, the swimmers jumped off the boats and started to swim back to land. It was so cold that some of the swimmers could not finish the race. The winner was Hungarian Alfréd Hajós, already the winner of the 100 metres swimming race.

At a dinner for the Olympic medallists, the King of Greece asked Hajós where he learned to swim so well.

'In the water,' answered the Hungarian.

The opening ceremony of the Athens Olympics of 1896

Of course, all the athletes at the first Games wanted to win their events. But it was also important to compete 'fairly'. For example, in the 100 kilometres bicycle race, a Greek rider stopped for repairs to his bicycle. The only other rider in the race – Léon Flameng of France – stopped and waited for him. When Flameng won the race, he was a popular winner with the crowd. Acts like this were good examples of Coubertin's ideas about sport.

● The longest race

The longest running race in the Olympics is the **marathon**. There was no race like this in the old Games. The race was named after a place in Greece. About 2,500 years ago, the Greek city of Athens was at war with Persia (now Iran). After the Athenians won an important fight against the Persians, a messenger, Pheidippides, ran a little more than 40 kilometres from the town of Marathon to Athens with the good news. He then fell down, dead.

Because the first modern Olympics were in Athens, one of Coubertin's friends suggested the idea of a marathon. Seventeen athletes – thirteen of them Greek – competed in the race. The crowds of 100,000 Greeks in and around the stadium were happy to see an athlete from their country, Spiridon Louis, come into the stadium first for the end of the race.

Louis won in less than three hours. Greek athletes crossed the finish line in second and third places too, but there was a problem about the man in third place. The facts were quickly discovered: the athlete rode part of the race in a vehicle!

The Games Continue

In general, the Games were thought to be a great success. Four years later, in 1900, the Olympics went to Coubertin's home city, Paris. For the first time, women could compete in some sports, but still not in running events.

Olympic Greats – Ray Ewry

American athlete Ray Ewry was one of the great athletes of the earliest modern Olympic Games. Between 1900 and 1908 he won eight gold medals in jumping events. At this time there were jumping events like the ones today, but there were also standing jumps. In these events athletes did not run before they jumped. They simply stood and then jumped. These standing jump events were stopped in 1912.

Ewry's great success was more special because of his early life. Before the Olympics, he was in a wheelchair for years. He could not stand or walk.

marathon /ˈmærəθən/ (n) a race on foot of about 42 kilometres

The next Olympics, in 1904, were in St Louis, in the United States. For the first time, the top three athletes in each event were given gold, silver and **bronze** medals. But these Games were not a great success. Not many athletes from outside North America travelled to St Louis. Even Coubertin did not go. The Games lasted from July until November, and so interest dropped.

Four years later, the Games returned to Europe. At the London Games of 1908, an important change was made to one of the Olympics' most famous races. In the first three Olympics, the **distance** of the marathon was not exactly the same. But the race organisers in London wanted the marathon to end right in front of the seat of Queen Alexandra, the wife of the British king. So they added a little distance to the race and made it 42.195 kilometres. This became the distance for all marathons.

Photographs of the end of the marathon in London became famous around the world. The first man into the stadium at the end of the race was an Italian called Dorando Pietri. (In the Olympics programme his name was listed as Pietri Dorando. Many people still know him as 'Dorando'.) But something was wrong. Pietri seemed to be in trouble. He started to run the wrong way. Games organisers showed him the right way, but the small runner was only able to go a few metres. Then he fell down on to the track. The crowd started to shout for him. Some wanted the organisers to help him. Others wanted them to leave the Italian.

But Pietri looked terrible. Nobody wanted him to die there on the track, in front of a crowd and the Queen! Doctors ran to help. Back on his feet, Pietri ran a few more metres. Then he fell again. This happened two more times. By now, another runner was inside the stadium, an American called John Hayes.

Just metres from the finish line, Pietri was starting to fall again. A race organiser caught the Italian and carried him across the finish line. That, of course, was against the rules. The gold medal was given to Hayes.

The next day, Pietri spoke to reporters. He was not happy about the race or about the help from the organisers and doctors. He did not receive a medal, but he was given a special gold cup by the Queen at a **ceremony** in the stadium. He immediately became famous all around the world.

● Not only sport

In the early days of the modern Olympics, there were some very different events. In one event at the St Louis Olympics, swimmers dived into the pool and swam

bronze /brɒnz/ (n) a metal, cheaper and darker than gold but a similar colour
distance /ˈdɪstəns/ (n) the amount of space between two places
ceremony /ˈserəməni/ (n) an important event where there are special, formal acts and words

under the water. The winner was the swimmer who went the greatest distance. This event was never repeated at the Olympics. It was too boring for the crowd!

At Stockholm in 1912, the organisers gave Olympic medals for art. For example, there were medals for music and painting. All the pieces of art were about sport in some way. These artistic events continued at the Olympics until 1948. One of the gold medallists at the 1912 Olympics won with a poem about sport. His name? Pierre de Coubertin! The father of the modern Olympic Games was also an Olympic winner.

But not all Coubertin's dreams became real. He wanted sport to bring an end to war, like the Olympics in Greece 2,000 years earlier. In the modern world, this was an impossible dream. The 1916 Games were planned for Berlin. But when World War I began, there could be no Olympics. The next Games were held in Antwerp in 1920, two years after the end of the war. There were also no Games in 1940 or 1944 because of World War II. But with these three exceptions, there has been an Olympic Games every four years since 1896.

Pietri is helped to the finish line at the 1908 Games.

2.1 Were you right?

Look back at your lists from Activity 1.2 on page iv. Then decide if these sentences are true (✓) or untrue (✗). Write the untrue sentences correctly below.

1 ☐ The early Olympics in Greece were held as often as the modern Olympics.

2 ☐ They were always held in a different city from the last Games.

3 ☐ Women competed only in the running events.

4 ☐ No woman could watch the Games.

5 ☐ Some of the events from those days are not held in the modern Olympics.

....

....

....

2.2 What more did you learn?

1 Choose a noun from box A and a verb from box B to complete each sentence below about the early modern Games.

| A land medal poem repairs rules |

| B jumped explained helped waited won |

a Coubertin ....explained.... five main .... for the modern Games.

b The swimmers .... off the boats and swam back to the

....

c One competitor stopped and .... for .... to another rider's bicycle.

d Pietri did not win the gold .... in the 1908 marathon because he was .... across the finish line.

e In 1912, Coubertin .... a gold medal for a .... about sport.

2 Discuss the three facts that you have found most interesting in these chapters.

2.3 Language in use

Read the sentences on the right. Then finish the sentences below with *could* or *had to*.

> Twenty athletes **could** run at the same time.
>
> Competitors **had to** be Greek-speakers and they **had to** be male.

1 Only unmarried women .... watch the early Olympic Games in Greece.

2 Wars between states .... stop during the Games.

3 In one race, runners .... carry heavy soldier's equipment.

4 Wars stopped so athletes .... travel safely to Olympia.

5 Fighters .... kick and break arms.

6 Runners .... run to one end of the track and then turn around.

7 In one race they .... go around the track 24 times.

8 Women .... only compete in the Games as horse owners.

2.4 What's next?

The following information is in Chapters 3 and 4. Match the dates with the sentences. What do you think?

1912	1924	1932	1936	1960	1984	1992	2008	2009

1 The first Winter Games were held. ....

2 Rio de Janeiro in Brazil was named the city to hold the 2016 Games. ....

3 Women swimmers first competed in the Olympics. ....

4 Only footballers under 23 could play in the Olympics. ....

5 The first Games for disabled athletes was held. ....

6 The women's marathon was introduced as an Olympic event. ....

7 The flame was first carried to the host city from Olympia. ....

8 For the first time, athletes stayed in an Olympic village. ....

CHAPTER 3

Open to All

It is possible that some great athletes never reached the Olympics because of Coubertin's rule about money.

In Pierre de Coubertin's opinion, international sport could make the world a better place. But he did not really want the Olympics to be open to *everybody*.

The Question of Money

Coubertin wanted no professional athletes to compete in the Games. In his opinion, athletes should compete only for the love of their sport. Athletes could not receive money for training or for winning their event.

Olympic Greats – Jim Thorpe

With two gold medals, the American Jim Thorpe was one of the stars of the 1912 Olympics in Stockholm. Some people even say that he was the greatest athlete of all time. This was the opinion of King Gustav V of Sweden. After the Games, the King said this to Thorpe. The athlete answered quietly, 'Thanks, King.'

But Thorpe's Olympic story ended sadly. When he was young, he played American ball games as a professional. The Olympic organisers found out about this and took his gold medals away. In 1983 – thirty years after Thorpe's death – the medals were given back to his family.

Some people think that Coubertin's view about money in sport was wrong. In their opinion, athletes have always needed time and equipment to train. This is very difficult if they have to work in another job. It is possible that some great athletes never reached the Olympics because of Coubertin's rule about money.

Then, after World War II, athletes from the Soviet Union (Russia and other smaller states) began to compete. The Soviet Union and Eastern European countries like East Germany spent a lot of money on sport. Successful athletes did not have to have other jobs; their sport *was* their job. To some people, these athletes were professionals.

From the 1970s, the rules about athletes and money started to change. Athletes could receive money and compete in the Games. The rules were different from event to event. For example, in football professionals could play at the Olympics from 1984, but not if they were in a World Cup team. In 1992, the rule for football changed again: after that time, only teams of players under the age of 23 could compete.

But in most events, professionals are now able to compete. If an athlete does well, he or she can earn large amounts of money after the Games from different businesses. More than one Olympic winner has had his or her face on packets of breakfast food!

Not Just for Men

Coubertin was not against the idea of sports for women, but he was not really interested in it. Female athletes did not compete in very many events in the first few modern Olympics. This changed slowly. In Stockholm in 1912, women swimmers competed for the first time. But the big change came in Amsterdam in 1928. In that year, women athletes ran in the 100 metres and the 800 metres, and also competed in the high jump and the discus.

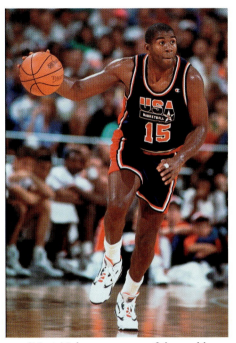

'Magic' Johnson was one of the world-famous professional basketball players in the 1992 Games.

Olympic Memories – The first female Olympic runner

At 16 years old, in 1928 the American Betty Robinson became the first woman star runner, in the 100 metres. Robinson was brought to the sport in an unusual way. She was a student at a school in Chicago. One day she was running to catch a train. One of her teachers noticed her speed. He asked her to train with the school's male runners. Only a few months later, she was in the Olympics final! Robinson was so nervous that she took the wrong shoes to the stadium: she almost ran in two left shoes.

In 1931, Robinson had a serious accident, and she was in a wheelchair for months. But Robinson worked and worked. Her body was never able again to get into the starting position for the 100 metres, but she could still run in the team 100 metres race. She did this at the 1936 Berlin Olympics, and she won another gold medal.

But many people were against the idea of women's track events. For them, the 800 metres final in 1928 proved that they were right. This race was won by the German, Lina Radke in a world-record time. But after the race, a few of the other runners fell to the ground. Doctors ran to help them. In the words of one British newspaper, the distance was 'too much for any girl'. Some people wanted to drop all women's events from the Olympics. Of course, male athletes sometimes fell to the ground after a race too. But it was a long time before women competed again in longer races at the Olympics. The next women's 800 metres event was in 1960, and other races were introduced much later:

- 1,500 metres 1972
- 10,000 metres 1988
- 3,000 metres and marathon 1984
- 5,000 metres 1996

Now women compete in almost all events at the Olympics, but more men than women still compete and, even now, some Olympic events are only for men.

But change continues. In Beijing in 2008, there were 11,196 athletes, and 4,746 of these were women – 42%, the highest number ever. In 2012, women boxers were able to compete for the first time. Until then, the sport was 'too dangerous' in the opinion of the Olympic organisers.

Olympic Greats – Babe Didrikson

The American Mildred 'Babe' Didrikson was probably the first big female star of the Olympics. At the Los Angeles Games in 1932, she was only eighteen, but she believed in herself strongly. She had good reason: 'Babe' was a natural athlete. She won gold medals in the javelin and the 80 metres hurdles. The high jump became a close competition between Didrikson and another American, Jean Shiley. Neither competitor seemed better than the other athlete, but then a judge ended Didrikson's hopes of a third gold medal. Her last jump – head first, like all of her jumps that day – was 'against the rules'. 'Babe' was given the silver medal.

CHAPTER 4

The Biggest Competition in the World

People in each city nervously wait to hear the news – will their country host the Olympic Games?

When people talk about 'the Olympics', they usually mean the 'Summer Olympics'. But there are two other Olympic Games. All together, these make the biggest sports competition in the world.

The Winter Olympics

In the very early modern Olympic Games, there were two events on ice – skating and ice hockey. But it was not possible to hold events on snow. For this reason, the first Winter Games were held in 1924, in Chamonix in France. In the same year, the Summer Olympics were held in Paris. Until 1992, the Summer and the Winter Olympics were held in the same year. But they were not always in the same country because, of course, not every country has the right cold weather for winter sports. Since 1994, organisers have held the Winter Olympics two years after the Summer Olympics. All the events are held on snow or ice.

Maria Riesch of Germany won two gold medals in the 2010 Games in Vancouver

The **host** city for the Winter Olympics must be in a cold place with enough snow and mountains for the Games. Cities in Europe, North America and Japan have hosted these Games. Of course, nobody can be sure about the weather. Days before the Vancouver Winter Olympics in 2010, the organisers were worried; with a warm winter in that part of Canada, there was not enough snow for the Games. Lorries had to carry snow from other parts of the country in time for the Games to begin.

Fewer countries send competitors to the Winter Olympics than to the Summer Olympics. Of course, most of the athletes come from colder countries that are known for winter sports. (It is difficult for a skier to practise in a flat, hot country!) But this is not always true. The Caribbean island of Jamaica – not exactly the home of winter sports – sent a four-man bobsleigh team to the Winter Olympics in Nagano, Japan, in 1998. They did not win but people loved the idea of a Jamaican bobsleigh team; there was even a popular film, *Cool Runnings*, about the team.

The Paralympics

In the first few modern Olympics, there were some athletes with disabilities. American **gymnast** George Eyser won six medals at the 1904 Games in St Louis, and three of these were gold. He was clearly one of the greatest gymnasts of the age. He also had only one leg: years before the Games, Eyser lost a leg in a train accident.

Since 1960, there have been Olympic Games that are specially for disabled athletes – the Paralympics. The first Paralympics were held in Rome. These Games were only open to athletes in wheelchairs, and

host /həʊst/ (n/v) the country or organisation that gives the space, buildings and equipment for a special event like a competition

gymnast /ˈdʒɪmnæst/ (n) an athlete who does skilful exercises and movements. The sport of **gymnastics** /dʒɪmˈnæstɪks/ has different events for men and women.

400 athletes from twenty-three countries competed. In 1976, new events for athletes with different disabilities were introduced. Since the 1988 Games in Seoul, the Paralympics have followed immediately after the Summer Olympics in the same host city. The Paralympics have grown and grown. At the 2008 Paralympics in Beijing, more than 3,900 athletes from 146 different countries competed.

The wheelchairs in the Paralympics are not like wheelchairs in daily life. They are built for speed. The fastest men's marathon in the 2008 Paralympics was a little more than one hour and twenty-three minutes; the winner of the men's marathon in the main Summer Olympics ran the distance in a much slower time of two hours, six minutes and thirty-two seconds.

The South African Oscar Pistorius is another great Paralympics athlete. After he lost both legs, he trained hard as a runner. He won world records at 100, 200 and 400 metres. Some people called him 'the fastest man on no legs'.

Pistorius started to run against athletes without disabilities. He wanted to compete in the main Summer Olympics in 2008. At first, the organisers said

Olympic Greats – Tanni Grey-Thompson

Britain's most famous athlete from the Paralympics is Tanni Grey-Thompson. She began wheelchair racing when she was only thirteen. At the age of nineteen, she won her first gold medal at the 1988 Paralympics in Seoul. Fours years later, in Barcelona, she won four gold medals; four years after *that*, she won one gold and three silver medals in Atlanta. In 2000, she was still racing: at Sydney she won another four gold medals. But even this was not the end. In the Athens Paralympics in 2004, she won two more gold medals at the age of thirty-five.

Oscar Pistorius, 'the fastest man on no legs'

no: in their opinion, it was unfair – not to Pistorius, but to the *other* athletes. They changed their mind about this, but Pistorius did not win a place on his country's Olympic team. He did win three gold medals at the Paralympics that year, and his dream of running in the main Olympics did not die.

The Host City

For each Games, cities from around the world compete to be the host city. Then the Olympics organisers (the IOC) choose the best place to host the Games. They want it to be the best for the events and the athletes and also for visitors to the Games. These cities wanted to host the 2016 Olympics:

The stadium in Beijing, 2008

- Chicago, US
- Tokyo, Japan
- Prague, Czech Republic
- Rio de Janeiro, Brazil

In 2009, people in each city nervously waited to hear the IOC's decision. It was Brazil. This will be the first time that a South American country has hosted the Games – 120 years after the first modern Olympics.

The host country and city need seven years to prepare for the Games. They know that the eyes of the world will be on them. They must build stadiums, swimming pools, and other buildings and outdoor areas for all the different events. The city must be ready for hundreds of thousands of visitors. Also, the competitors need somewhere to live. Since the Los Angeles Games of 1932, the host city has built a special Olympic village for all the athletes.

Of course, it costs a lot of money to host the biggest sports competition in the world. It took the people of Canada twenty years to pay for the 1976 Olympics in Montreal. But the Olympics can bring a lot of money and business to its host city and country. Today big businesses often give money to the Games because they can reach a market of customers all around the world. TV companies also pay to show the Olympics in their countries.

After the Games, the new stadiums and sports areas can be used by the local people. In this way, the host city can use the Games to help poorer areas. For example, the organisers of the 2012 London Olympics decided to hold many of the events in a poor area in the east of the city.

● The centre of the Games

Probably the most important place in the host city for each Games is the main stadium. People all around the world remember the wonderful stadium at the Beijing Olympics in 2008.

The Games always start with an opening ceremony in the main stadium. In Beijing, 91,000 people in the stadium – and about four billion people around the world – watched the opening ceremony. The show had music, lights and dance. There were 15,000 people in it – more than the number of athletes at the Games!

During every opening ceremony, competitors from every country in the Games come into the stadium. The Greek team always comes first. After that, teams from all the other countries come into the stadium in order, from A to Z.

One of the most important parts of the opening ceremony is the lighting of the Olympic **flame**. This flame burns all through the Olympic Games (usually about two weeks), but this was not always part of the opening ceremony. The first Olympic Games with the Olympic flame was Amsterdam in 1928. Then, at the Berlin Games in 1936, the organisers had a new idea. The Olympic flame was carried from Olympia – the home of the old Olympic Games in Greece – all the way to the host city. This still happens. Usually a small flame is passed from person to person along the way. Finally, in the stadium, the last holder of the smaller flame lights the main Olympic flame. This important job can be done in lots of wonderful ways.

Olympic Memories – The wrong flame!

Before the 1956 Olympics in Melbourne, Australia, the Olympic flame travelled across Australia. Large crowds and local politicians were waiting in Sydney. But some students decided to play a joke. They made a new Olympic flame using a long stick and some old, burning clothes. When one of them arrived with this in the streets of Sydney, the crowds shouted for him. With the wrong flame in his hand, a local politician gave a speech to the large crowd. When the real Olympic flame arrived hours later, most of the crowd was not there!

flame /fleɪm/ (n) hot, burning gas that you can see, from a fire

3.1 Were you right?

Look at your answers to Activity 2.4. Then cross out the mistakes in these sentences and write the correct words.

1 Women ~~runners~~ first competed in the 1912 Games.   *swimmers*

2 The rules changed for professional footballers in the 1970s and then again in the 1990s.   ....

3 After the 1928 marathon, there were no women's long distance races for a long time.   ....

4 The first Winter Games were held in 1924 because earlier Olympics could not have events on ice.   ....

5 The first Paralympics were held in Chamonix in 1960.   ....

6 Rio de Janeiro had nine years to prepare the city for the 2016 Olympics.   ....

7 The opening ceremony is always held in the Olympic Village.   ....

8 The Olympic flame was introduced in Berlin.   ....

3.2 What more did you learn?

Circle the correct information.

1 Jim Thorpe's medals were taken away because he

   a was rude to the king of Sweden.   **b** played professional sports.

2 After an accident in 1931, Betty Robinson

   a never ran again.   **b** competed again in the Olympics.

3 When Babe Didrikson competed in the 1932 Games, she won

   a two gold medals.   **b** three gold medals.

4 In the 1998 Winter Olympics, a bobsleigh team from Jamaica

   a competed.   **b** won gold medals.

5 At the opening ceremony, the first team into the stadium are from

   a Greece.   **b** the host country.

.3 Language in use

Read the sentences on the right. Then finish each sentence below with the correct present perfect form of a verb from the box.

host	grow	hold	bring
change	compete	decide	

Since the 1988 Games in Seoul, the Paralympics **have followed** immediately after the Summer Olympics.

Since 1994, organisers **have held** the Winter Olympics two years after the Summer Olympics.

1   The rules about money for athletes .... since the first Olympics.

2   The Olympic organisers .... finally .... to have women's boxing as an event.

3   The organisers .... always .... the Winter Olympics in cold countries.

4   More than once, the organisers .... snow to the host city for the Winter Games.

5   The Paralympics .... bigger and bigger over the years.

6   An African city .... never .... the Olympic Games.

7   More and more women .... in the last few Games.

.4 What's next?

Match the questions with the correct countries. What do you think?

1   Which country sent no athletes to the 1984 Los Angeles Games?

2   Which country received the most medals in 2008?

3   Which country received the most medals in Berlin in 1936?

4   A team from which country lost a basketball final and then refused to receive their medals?

5   Which country brought problems to the Olympics because it sent a sports team to play in South Africa?

a   United States

b   Germany

c   Soviet Union

d   New Zealand

e   China

CHAPTER 5

Nation against Nation

At every Olympic Games, people all around the world look at these tables carefully. Which country is winning?

The Olympics have become more international with every Games. At the first modern Olympics, there were athletes from only fourteen countries, all from Europe or North America. By 1936, there were forty-nine countries at the Games; by 1968 there were teams from more than 100 countries for the first time. At Beijing in 2008, 204 countries sent athletes.

At the same time, more countries wanted to host the Olympics too. In 1956, they were held in Melbourne, Australia. The first Asian Olympics were in Tokyo in 1964; the Games returned to Asia in 1988 (Seoul) and 2008 (Beijing).

The Medals Table

Under the rules of the Olympics, the Games are competitions between athletes, not between countries. This idea was very important to Pierre de Coubertin. Until 1908, athletes did not even compete in the Games as part of a national team.

But the athletes' nationality quickly became very important at the Games. In the opening ceremony, athletes from each country now come into the stadium behind their nation's **flag**. The athletes are proud to compete in their nation's colours. And if they win a gold medal, their national **anthem** is played at the ceremony. Success at the Olympic Games is very important to governments around the world. The clearest sign of this success is a country's position in the medals table. At every Olympic Games, people all around the world look at these tables carefully. Which country is winning? Usually a country's position is decided by the number of gold medals, not the total number of medals.

A look at the medals tables through the years shows big changes. Athletes from the United States won the most gold medals at the first Games in 1896. Then, in all the Games before World War I, the top ten countries in the medals table were from Europe or North America. In the four Olympic Games from 1900-1912, the host country was always top of the medals table. After World War I, the US won every Olympic Games until 1952, except one – the host nation, Germany, took the most gold medals at the Olympic Games in Berlin in 1936.

---

flag /flæg/ (n) a piece of cloth with colours or pictures on it that is the sign of a country
anthem /ˈænθəm/ (n) the song that is played for a country at events like international sports competitions

Olympic Facts – Gold medals

An Olympic gold medal must have six grams or more of real gold in it. Of course, every athlete at the Games wants to win a gold medal. In the 1956 Games in Melbourne, one young athlete from the Soviet Union showed how important the medal was to him. He won a gold for an event on the water. He jumped up happily and threw his new medal up into the air. He failed to catch it and the medal fell into the lake behind him. The athlete dived in but was unable to find it. The organisers of the Melbourne Games gave him a second medal. The same athlete won gold medals at the 1960 and 1964 Games too. He was more careful with those!

● The 'Cold War'

After World War II, other countries moved up the medals table: for example, Japan was often near the top. But the biggest change came when the Soviet Union began to send athletes. From the 1950s, the Soviet Union and the United States had very different forms of government and ways of life. For years there was worry about a war between the two countries. This never happened, but each country tried to look stronger than the other in smaller ways. International sport was one of these ways. Each country wanted to be top of the Olympic medals table. For people on both sides, success at the Olympics was more than just success in sport; it was success for that country's way of life and government. Of course, not all Olympic athletes felt this way about the 'war'. After the 1976 Montreal Games, the American swimmer John Naber spoke about his gold medal: 'It means I swam faster ... that's all.'

Two famous team games really showed how important Olympic success was to the United States and the Soviet Union:

1972 basketball final:

From the first basketball game at the Olympics in 1932, the US team won gold medal after gold medal. They did not lose even one game. But in Munich in 1972, they met the Soviet team in the final. It was a close and hard game. When the sound came for the end of the game, the US were winning by 50 points to 49. But there was a problem – a mistake with the clock. Three more seconds were added to the game. In those three seconds, the Soviet team **scored**. Now *they* were the winners, by 51 points to 50! The US team could not believe this. They were so angry that they refused to receive their silver medals at the medal ceremony.

score /skɔː/ (v/n) to win a point in a game. The **score** shows the total number of points for each side.

1980 ice hockey game:

In 1980, the Soviet ice hockey team was the best in the world. But the young team from the US – many of them students at university – were ready for the 1980 Olympics in Lake Placid. On the day of the game, their trainer told them, 'You are *meant* to be here at this time.' With his words in their ears, the team played their best game ever. With only ten minutes before the end of the game, they were winning. The players from the Soviet Union attacked again and again, but they could not score. The win was big news in the United States. The American team still had to meet Finland in the final. They did and they won that game too. But their real success was against the Soviet Union.

From 1991, the Soviet Union was not a single nation; its different parts became their own countries again. But in the 1992 Olympics, the old countries of the Soviet Union still competed as one nation. They were top of the medal table too. In the Olympics after that, they competed as different countries.

But soon the medal table was not just a fight between the United States and Russia. China hosted the Olympic Games, for the first time, in 2008. The country wanted to show the world how successful modern China was. At the end of the Games, China was at the top of the medal table, with fifty-one gold medals. The US was second (with a higher total number of medals), and Russia was third.

Sending a Message

At different times in the history of the modern Olympics, some countries have chosen not to send athletes. They wanted to send a message to the world.

- In 1972, more than twenty nations – most of them from Africa – refused to send athletes to the Games. They were angry because a team from New Zealand was competing in the Games. (Before the Games, New Zealand sent a sports team to play against South Africa. At that time, most countries refused to play any sports with South Africa until that country gave more rights to its black people.)
- In 1980, the Games were held in Moscow, the capital of the Soviet Union. It was a year after the Soviet Union sent soldiers into Afghanistan. Because of this, the US, Japan, China and West Germany refused to send athletes to the Moscow Games. In some countries, like Britain and Australia, athletes could make their own decision. In the end, teams from eighty nations competed in the Games.
- Four years later, the Soviet Union did not forget what happened in 1980. It and other Eastern European countries refused to send athletes to the Los Angeles Games. In total, fourteen countries did not compete.

The Worst Time

The worst time at the Olympics came in Munich in 1972. On 5 September, a group of Palestinians attacked the team from Israel in the Olympic village. They killed two of the athletes and held nine other athletes. When the German police tried to free the Israelis, the athletes were killed. Five of the attackers and one policeman died too. It was a terrible time for the Olympics, but the organisers decided to continue with the Munich Games.

Olympic Memories – An angry message

Sometimes athletes, not nations, used the Games to send a message. At Mexico City in 1968, the American runner Tommie Smith won the 200 metres race. Another American, John Carlos, was third. Both men were black Americans. During the medal ceremony, they wore no shoes on their feet as a sign of how poor many black Americans were. As the US national anthem played, each man put his head down and one hand up in the air. They were angry about life in the United States for black Americans and they wanted to tell the world.

In the US, many people were angry. In their opinion, this action was against the idea of the Olympic Games. To others, the two athletes were bravely sending an important message about real problems in their country.

CHAPTER 6

Higher and Longer

Photographs of the final are hard to believe. At the highest point of his long jump, Beamon almost reached his own height!

Coubertin's description of the Olympics in three words was 'faster, higher, stronger'. No event is a better example of the second of these words than the high jump. The usual body type for this event is tall and thin.

One of the most famous high jumpers in the event's history gave his name to a kind of jump. During the 1968 high jump final, all eyes in the stadium were on one man, the American Dick Fosbury. Before Fosbury, all high jumpers jumped in the same way, with one foot over the bar first. Fosbury changed everything. He worked on a new kind of jump, with his head over first and his back to the bar. It was successful but, to many people, it looked (in Fosbury's word) 'funny'. He won a place on the American Olympic team, but not as the country's best high jumper. But then at the Olympics final, 80,000 people in the stadium watched as Fosbury won the gold medal with his strange new jump.

After Fosbury's win, one of the organisers of the American team was still unhappy about the new jump: 'If children copy this, they will break their necks.' But slowly other high jumpers changed to the new way. In the 1980 Olympics in Moscow, thirteen of the sixteen competitors used Fosbury's way of jumping.

Fosbury's new jump in 1968

A Jump into History

1968 was an important year for another Olympic jumping event – the long jump. At the Mexico Games, Bob Beamon did not compete very well in the early part of the competition; he just got into the finals. He was tall – about 1.9 m – and very fast, but he sometimes had trouble with the start of his jump. Nobody had much hope for the 22-year-old American. But he had no trouble in the long jump final in 1968. He jumped perfectly. Photographs of the final are hard to believe. At the highest point of his jump Beamon almost reached his own height! He then landed almost out of the sand. The crowd understood immediately: this was a *very* long jump. Then they saw the distance on the electronic sign – 8.9 metres, more than 0.4 metres longer than the last

record. It was hard to believe, even for Beamon. He was as surprised as anyone. One of the other jumpers, British athlete Lynn Davies, did not want to continue with the event that day. He said to another competitor, 'What is the point? We'll all look silly.' Then Davies said these famous words to the new record-holder: 'You have destroyed this event.'

Bob Beamon's world-record jump

For many years, Davies's words seemed to be true. Nobody could jump farther than Beamon's jump that day. But at last in 1991 – twenty-three years later – Beamon's world record was broken (but not in the Olympics). Beamon took the news well: 'I don't feel any different,' he said.

At the 1996 Games in Atlanta, Nigerian long jumper Chioma Ajunwa was a surprise winner in the women's event – a surprise to herself. She came to the Games to run in the 100 metres, but did not do well. Then the Nigerian trainers told her their new plan: she was competing in the long jump too! She jumped the farthest in the event and became the first Nigerian medallist in any sport.

In the same year, the American Carl Lewis added the gold medal for the long jump to his gold medals for the same event from *three* earlier Olympic Games. Before he left the field in Atlanta, he picked up some sand from the long jump. He wanted to keep it as a memory of his success.

The Longest Jump

One of the most popular events at the Winter Olympics is the ski jumping competition. In this event, points are given for the distance of each jump; judges also give the jumpers points for the skill of the jump.

Before 1985, competitors jumped with their skis straight. At about that time, a Swedish athlete started to place his skis in the shape of a letter V. At first, people laughed at this strange new way of jumping; judges gave it low points. But soon it became clear: competitors could jump much higher with their skis in this shape. By the 1992 Olympics, all the medallists used the V shape in the ski jumping event.

Ski-jumpers can fly at speeds of 95 kilometres an hour.

Many people hoped for a women's ski-jumping event in the 2010 Winter Games in Vancouver. The Olympic organisers said no. Many people still can not understand their reasons.

Throwing Events

Athletes in the Olympic throwing events also try to go 'longer' than their competitors. Two of these events – the javelin and the discus – were events in the early Olympic Games in Greece too.

● Javelin

In many Olympic events, new equipment makes athletes better and better. This was true for the javelin. When athletes changed from wood to metal javelins, distances in the event were soon longer.

But there was a problem: the point on the end of a javelin is sharp. With longer and longer throws, the event was becoming dangerous. Finally, the sport's organisers decided to change the weight and shape of the javelin again. For the men's event, they did this in 1986. With the new javelin, throws were shorter. Of course, this was not fair to athletes who wanted to break world and Olympic records. The answer was easy: the sport's organisers started again with new records for the new javelin. The same thing happened for the women's javelin event in 1999, in time for the 2000 Olympics.

● Discus

American Al Oerter was one of the greatest discus throwers ever. He won Olympic gold in the event four times, in 1956, 1960, 1964 and 1968. The third competition, at the Tokyo Games, was the hardest. Oerter was in a lot of pain before the Games. Doctors told him not to compete, but Oerter did not listen. With his fifth throw in the final, he almost fell over with the pain. But the throw was a new world-record distance. After the event, Oerter explained: 'These are the Olympics. You die for them.'

Discus thrower Al Oerter

29

4.1 Were you right?

Look at your answers to Activity 3.4. Then discuss these statements.
What do you think?

> Sport is not the business of politicians.

> Governments can use sport to send important messages to other governments.

4.2 What more did you learn?

Match the newspaper stories with the subjects.

A **An angry message home**

D **'You have destroyed this event!'**

B **Seventeen are killed at the Games**

E **No to women jumpers again**

C **New jump is a winner**

F **Pain cannot stop big Al winning gold**

1 ☐ ski jumping at the 2010 Winter Olympics

2 ☐ attack on the Israeli team at the Munich Games

3 ☐ Tommie Smith and John Carlos at the medal ceremony

4 ☐ Bob Beamon's long jump in 1968

5 ☐ discus thrower Oerter

6 ☐ Dick Fosbury's high jump in 1968

4.3 Language in use

Look at the sentences on the right. Then rewrite these sentences using passive verb forms.

> Usually a country's position **is decided** by the number of gold medals.
>
> Three more seconds **were added** to the game.

1 The organisers play the gold medallist's national anthem during the ceremony.

   The gold medallist's national anthem is played during the ceremony.

2 The IOC chooses the host city seven years before the Games.

3 The organisers of the Melbourne Games gave the athlete a new gold medal.

4 The Soviet Union did not send athletes to the 1984 Olympics.

5 The police killed five of the attackers at the Munich Olympics.

6 Fosbury's new way of jumping completely changed the event.

4.4 What's next?

Match the Olympic runners with the questions below. Write the letters A–D.

1 ☐ Who proved Hitler wrong?

2 ☐ Who called himself 'lazy'?

3 ☐ Who was called the 'Daughter of the Wind'?

4 ☐ Whose success on the track seemed very sudden?

A Usain Bolt

B Jesse Owens

C Florence Griffith-Joyner

D Naoko Takahashi

CHAPTER 7

Run, Run, Run!

In the 100 metres final, Bolt even hit his own chest and lowered his arms 15 metres from the finish line. He was the winner and he already knew it!

The first event in the Greek Olympics thousands of years ago was a race on foot. The opening event of the first modern Olympics was a foot race too.

The Fastest in the World

The 200 metres and 400 metres races are both exciting, but for many people there is something special about the shortest and fastest race of all, the men's 100 metres. The holder of the world record in this event can call himself 'the fastest man in the world'. The winner of the gold medal for this event in 1896 went to American Thomas Burke. He won with a time of 12 seconds exactly. But soon athletes were running a lot faster than this.

● The man who proved Hitler wrong

One of the most famous speed athletes in Olympic history was American Jesse Owens. He already held three world records when he went to the eleventh Olympic Games in Berlin in 1936. At these Games, Adolf Hitler wanted to prove the Nazis' idea that white athletes were better than other athletes. Owens, an African American, destroyed this idea with gold medals in four events – the 100 metres, the 200 metres, the long jump and the men's 4x100 metres – and his wins looked *easy*! After the Games, a reporter asked Owens to explain the secret of his success. 'My feet spend as little time as possible on the ground,' the athlete answered.

● New records

Owens won his 100 metres final in a time of 10.3 seconds. But in following years, speed athletes had their eyes on a new record: each wanted to be the first man ever to complete the 100 metres in under ten seconds. 'Impossible!' cried many people, but with each new record, runners were coming a little nearer to this 'impossible' dream. At the Tokyo Olympics in 1964, the event was won in 10 seconds exactly. Then at the Mexico City Olympics in 1968, the American James Hines went *under* 10 seconds with a world-record time of 9.95 seconds.

Of course, in a race like the 100 metres, the difference between winning and losing can be very small. In the final in Athens in 2004, there was just 0.01 of a second between gold and silver. It is very important to have electronic equipment to record these times exactly. Other equipment checks how strong the wind is. If there is a wind of more than 2 metres a second behind the runners, the race time cannot be counted as an Olympic record.

Where will it end? Will anybody ever run 100 metres in under nine seconds? Of course, people now say that *this* is an impossible dream. But every year, little by little, athletes record faster times …

Olympic Greats – Usain Bolt

At a height of almost 1.96 metres, Jamaican Usain Bolt is taller than most other runners in his event. At the Beijing Olympics in 2008, his trainer did not want Bolt to run the 100 metres; in his opinion, the runner should only compete in his 'best event', the 200 metres. In the end, Bolt ran in both races. He won gold medals *and* broke the world record in both. In the 100 metres final, Bolt even hit his own chest and lowered his arms 15 metres from the finish line. He was the winner and he already knew it! Bolt won a third gold medal at Beijing as part of Jamaica's men's 4x100 metres team. But in magazines and newspapers, he has described himself as 'lazy'!

● **The fastest women**

There have been many great women Olympic athletes at short distances too.

Fanny Blankers-Koen

One of the greatest was Fanny Blankers-Koen from the Netherlands. She first competed in the 1936 Olympics at the age of eighteen, but she did not win a medal. Because of World War II, there were no Olympic Games for the next twelve years. By the time of the 1948 Games in London, Blankers-Koen was thirty, a mother of two children. Was she too old? The answer was a loud 'No!' Fanny won four gold medals in London – for the 100 metres and 200 metres, the 80 metres hurdles and the long jump. When she went home, she was a big star in the Netherlands. Her neighbours gave her a special present – a bicycle. They did not want her to 'have to run so much'.

Flojo

The world knew the American athlete Florence Griffith-Joyner as 'Flojo'. Before 1988, she was a successful athlete, but not a great one. Then everything changed. She ran the 100 metres in 10.49 seconds. This was a lot faster than her earlier times; it was faster than many top male athletes at that time. A lot of people were very surprised. But at the Seoul Olympics, Flojo was almost as fast. She won the 100 metres final with a time of 10.54 seconds (with wind), and she won the 200 metres with a world-record time of 21.34 seconds. By the 2008 Olympics twenty years later, Flojo's 1988 times were still records.

But for some people there was a shadow over Flojo's success. How did she become much faster so quickly in 1988? 'Did she use **drugs**?' some people thought. This talk continued after Flojo's sudden death at the young age of thirty-eight.

In the Middle

The 800 metres and 1,500 metres are usually called 'middle-distance' races. For both distances, runners must plan their race carefully. Some athletes try to reach the front early and stay there until the end. Others prefer to wait behind the athlete at the front and then find more speed for the last part of the race.

One of the greatest middle-distance runners was Kip Keino. The Kenyan athlete was also a long-distance runner. At the Mexico City Games in 1968, he was already the silver medallist for the 5,000 metres when it was time for the 1,500 metres final. But Keino was not feeling well that day. Also, the traffic near the stadium was terrible. He did not want to miss the race, so Keino

---

drug /drʌg/ (n) something that makes athletes stronger or faster. It is against the rules of competitions like the Olympics for athletes to take drugs.

jumped out of the vehicle and ran to the stadium on foot. In the race, he forgot all these problems and won the gold medal easily against the world record holder.

Kip Keino winning the 1,500 metres race in Mexico in 1968

Long Distance

Long-distance races are the 5,000 metres, the 10,000 metres and the marathon. Of course, like all athletes, successful long-distance runners must have a strong body, but they must have a strong mind too. The Finnish athlete Paavo Nurmi from the 1920s understood this: in his own words, his success on the track was

Olympic Greats – Emil Zátopek

One of the greatest long-distance runners ever was Emil Zátopek from Czechoslovakia (later the Czech Republic and Slovakia). Between 1948 and 1954, he ran in thirty-eight 10,000 metre races and did not lose one. He did not always seem happy during races; his face sometimes had a look of pain. 'I cannot run and smile at the same time,' Zátopek explained.

At the 1952 Helsinki Games, Zátopek won the 5,000 metres and 10,000 metres. He knew very little about the marathon, but he decided to run in that too. After 9 kilometres, he asked another runner about the speed: was it OK? The other runner replied, 'No, it's too slow.' This was not really true: he wanted Zátopek to get tired. But the Czech runner did not know this. He simply ran faster, all the way to the finish line and another gold medal!

'because of my mind'.

In the early Olympics, Finland produced many great long-distance runners – twenty-four gold medals between 1912 and 1932. Nurmi was the most famous of them all. Between 1920 and 1928, he won nine gold medals. Sometimes Nurmi even raced with a watch to check his own speed. He did this because other athletes did not come near him.

Finland had to wait a long time for its next really great long-distance runner, Lasse Virén. Virén fell during the final of the 10,000 metres at Munich in 1972. He got to his feet and won his first gold medal in a world-record time.

Naoko Takahashi, winner of the Women's Marathon in 2000, was Japan's first gold medallist in a running event. At home she was called 'Daughter of the Wind'.

● Africa on top

Since 1960, African runners have won many long-distance races at the Olympics. This started at the Games in Rome. The athletes ran at night so the temperature was not so high. For Ethiopian runner Abebe Bikila, this was only the third marathon in his life. He ran without shoes and he won the gold medal. After the race, he was asked why he did not wear shoes. Bikila answered, 'We train in shoes. But it's much more comfortable to run without them.' (The Olympic organisers were surprised by Bikila's win. The stadium musicians did not know the Ethiopian national anthem, so they played the Italian anthem!) Bikila was the first black African to win an Olympic gold medal, and many followed him. In the 1968 Mexico City Olympics, African runners took gold medals in every men's race from the 1,500 metres up to the marathon.

Kenya and Ethiopia continue to produce wonderful middle and long-distance runners: at the Beijing Games in 2008, Kenyan athletes won the men's 800 metres, 1,500 metres and marathon, and the women's 800 metres and 1,500 metres; Ethiopian athletes won the men's and women's 5,000 metres and 10,000 metres.

CHAPTER 8

Faster and Faster

People could not believe British rider Chris Boardman's bicycle. It looked like something from the future!

Of course, races on foot are not the only races at the Olympics. The Games have had races on bicycles, boats, skis and skates, and races in the water.

On Two Wheels

Before 1996, there were two main kinds of Olympic bicycle race – road races outside and races on an inside track. At the Atlanta Games, a race for mountain bikes was introduced. In the same year, professional riders competed in the Games for the first time. In the 2008 Olympics, there was a fourth kind of bicycle race. Of course, a rider's bicycle is very important in competitions like the Olympics. Very different types of bike are needed for the different events.

Olympic Memories – The bicycle from the future

People could not believe British rider Chris Boardman's bicycle. It looked like something from the future! It was built by a team who usually make racing cars. At the time – the Barcelona Games in 1992 – it was the fastest and (at only 9 kilos) the lightest bicycle ever. Even Boardman's hat was a special shape to help him to go faster.

Boardman won the gold medal easily. The silver medallist, the German Jens Lehmann, was not angry about Boardman's bicycle. In his words, 'the man, not the machine' won the gold medal. (And years later, Boardman broke the world record again on an 'old' kind of bike.)

Other Races

- The fastest speeds in a race are in the downhill skiing at the Winter Olympics. Skiers can reach speeds of over 130 kilometres an hour.
- There are also skating races at the Winter Games. American Eric Heiden was one of the greatest speed skaters ever. He won gold medals in all five of the men's speed-skating races at the 1980 Winter Games.
- There have been Olympic boat races since the second modern Olympics in 1900. Some of these are held at sea; others are held on lakes and on rivers.

German Birgit Fischer competed on the water in six different Olympics.

In the pool

From the speed of the 50 metres race to the long-distance 10,000 metres race, many of the Olympics' greatest stories are in the pool. But who is the best swimmer ever? This is a difficult question. How do you judge? By the number of medals in one Games or in different Olympics? Here are some swimmers who have held the title of 'best swimmer ever' at different times.

Johnny Weissmüller

Born in Romania, Johnny Weissmüller moved to the United States as a child. Later in life, he competed for his new country. He became the first man to swim 100 metres in less than a minute. At the Paris Olympics in 1924, he won three gold medals. Tall and good-looking, he was very popular with the French crowds; he and another athlete did funny diving shows for the crowds between races. Weissmüller won a gold medal again in Amsterdam four years later, but he was already planning a different kind of life. After his last swimming competition, he went to Hollywood. Weissmüller became famous as Tarzan. (Three other Olympic medallists also played the part of Tarzan in different films. This part probably needed more swimming than acting skills!)

Mark Spitz

For years, Mark Spitz from the US was remembered as the best Olympic swimmer ever. He won seven gold medals for swimming at the 1972 Games in Munich, all in world-record times. When he was little, his father taught Spitz an important lesson: 'Swimming isn't everything,' his father said. 'Winning is.'

Michael Phelps

But in 2008, another American swimmer did better even than Mark Spitz. His name was Michael Phelps. He already had a great Olympic history, with six gold medals and two bronze medals at the Athens Olympics in 2004. But in Beijing, Phelps swam in seventeen races in nine days, and won them all. He came away with eight gold medals – more than any other Olympic athlete at the same Games. But it was not always easy. Phelps won his seventh gold by just 0.01 of a second! Phelps said about his success, 'Dream as big as you can dream, and anything is possible.' Mark Spitz described Phelps as not only 'the greatest swimmer of all time', but maybe 'the greatest athlete of all time.'

Michael Phelps

Olympic Greats – Dawn Fraser

Australia has a long history of success in the Olympic swimming pool. One of the country's most famous swimmers is Dawn Fraser. She was only nineteen when she won a gold medal for the 100 metres in her home country in 1956. She won a gold medal again four years later in Rome, and then again four years after that in Tokyo. By this time, she was twenty-seven – quite old for an Olympic swimmer.

In Tokyo, the Australian team told Fraser not to go to the opening ceremony; they wanted her to rest. Fraser had other ideas. She went and enjoyed the start of her third Games. After she won her medal, Fraser got into more trouble in Tokyo. As a joke, she and some friends went to a palace in the city in the middle of the night to steal a flag. The plan failed and the police caught Fraser. Luckily the swimmer did not have to go to court. The Japanese government even gave the flag to Fraser to remember her time in Tokyo.

5.1 Were you right?

Look back at your answers to Activity 4.4. Then write the correct names below.

1 He won gold medals at the Berlin Olympics.   ....

2 Her neighbours gave her a funny present.   ....

3 He won three gold medals but called himself 'lazy'.   ....

4 Some people were surprised when her times became much faster. ....

5 He was almost late for an Olympic race.   ....

6 He said, 'I cannot run and smile.'   ....

7 She 'ran like the wind' to win Japan's first gold medal for running. ....

8 He ran the marathon with no shoes.   ....

5.2 What more did you learn?

Complete the table.

Name	Nationality	Event(s)	Interesting fact
Mark Spitz	US	....	He learned important lessons about winning from his ....
Chris Boardman	....	cycling	He rode an unusual kind of ....
....	Australia	swimming	She got into trouble with a joke at the .... Olympics.
Michael Phelps	US	....	He became the athlete with the most gold .... in the same Games.
Fanny Blankers-Koen	....	100 m, 200 m, 80m hurdles, ...	She was a mother of .... children when she won four gold medals.
....	....	swimming	He became a film star.

5.3 Language in use

Look at the sentences on the right. Then match the sentence halves below.

> It is very **important to have** electronic equipment to record these times exactly.
>
> 'We train in shoes. But it's much **more comfortable to run** without them.'

1 In the opinion of many people, it was impossible ☑ f

2 Michael Phelps was proud ☐

3 People were pleased ☐

4 Unfortunately for some athletes, it is not easy ☐

5 If you want to win, it is necessary ☐

6 After years of training, she is ready ☐

a to see Weissmüller as Tarzan.   **b** to train hard.   **c** to win so many gold medals

d to say no to drugs.   **e** to try and break the record.

f for anyone to run 100 metres in under 10 seconds.

5.4 What's next?

Which of these sentences are right (R)? Which are wrong (W)? What do you think?

1 If two weightlifters have lifted exactly the same weight, they both receive the same medal. ☐

2 In the early modern Olympics, wrestling fights could be very long. ☐

3 The rules of Olympic boxing are different from the rules for professional boxing. ☐

4 The boxer Muhammad Ali was a Muslim when he competed in the Olympics. ☐

5 The gymnast Nadia Comăneci received the first 'perfect score' in any gymnastics event. ☐

CHAPTER 9

Stronger

'This is not my gold medal!' Süleymanoğlu told the crowd.
'This is the Turkish people's medal!'

For many Olympic events it is important to be strong. One event is the clearest test of this – weightlifting.

The Strongest of the Strong

In one weightlifting event in the first few Games, athletes had to lift weights with one hand! Now there are two kinds of lifts (both with two hands). The points from the two best lifts are added together. The winner is the athlete with the highest total number of points.

The lifter's own weight can be very important in this event. Lifters compete in different weight groups. Before the competition, they are weighed. Sometimes it is difficult for an athlete to reach the correct weight. In 1956, in Melbourne, the American weightlifter Charles Vinci was a little too heavy for his weight group. He went away and ran for an hour. After this, he was still too heavy. At the last minute, Vinci's team cut most of his hair off! The plan worked. Vinci competed and won a gold medal, with a new world-record.

If two weightlifters have lifted exactly the same weight, the judges look at the weight of the athletes. In Melbourne Paul Anderson of the US and Humberto Selvetti of Argentina both had a total of exactly 500 kilos, an Olympic record. Anderson received the gold medal because he weighed 5.6 kilos

Olympic Greats – Naim Süleymanoğlu

Süleymanoğlu was born in Bulgaria, but his parents were Turkish. As a young man he was not tall – less than 1.5 metres – but he was *strong*. At the age of fourteen, he almost broke the adult world record for weightlifting at his weight.

In the 1988 Seoul Olympics, he was part of the Turkish team. His gold medal was the country's first for twenty years. Süleymanoğlu lifted a heavier total weight than the gold medallist in the *heaviest* group in 1956, Paul Anderson. Anderson weighed 137 kilos, and Süleymanoğlu just 60.

After his last lift in Seoul, Süleymanoğlu kissed the metal bar goodbye. He did not plan to continue in the sport. But on his return to Turkey, about one million people were waiting for him in the Turkish capital, Ankara. 'This is not my gold medal!' Süleymanğoglu told the crowd. 'This is the Turkish people's medal!' He decided to compete again and he repeated his gold medal success in Barcelona and Atlanta.

less than Selvetti. The American athlete felt lucky: months before, he was 25 kilos *heavier*.

The first women's weightlifting event was held in Sydney in 2000. In the 2008 Games in Beijing, the winner in the heaviest group was the South Korean Jang Mi-Ran. She broke the world record for both kinds of lift and for the total weight – 326 kilos. In one of her lifts, she lifted 186 kilos over her head.

*Jang Mi-Ran at the
2008 Games*

Fighting Sports

Athletes in fighting sports are strong, but of course successful fighters have skill and speed too. There are a few fighting events in the modern Olympics.

● Wrestling

There are two different kinds of wrestling. In one of them, it is possible for a wrestler to use his legs more in moves. In the other event, a fighter cannot push, press or lift the other fighter with his legs.

Today, fights are not very long – two halves of three minutes each. But in the early days of the Olympics, it was very different. In one fight at the 1912 Olympics in Stockholm, the fighters – one from Sweden and one from Finland – fought for *nine hours*! They were still wrestling when the judges ended the fight. Neither man was given a gold medal; they both received silver.

Probably the greatest wrestler of the modern Olympics was the Russian Alexander Medved. Some people say that he was the greatest wrestler of all time. The best wrestlers have to think and act quickly. Nobody did this better than Medved. He won gold medals at three Olympic Games, between 1964 and 1972. He often won against bigger fighters.

● Boxing

Olympic boxing is a little different from professional boxing. The fights are shorter, and boxers have protection on their heads.

Boxing is the only Olympic sport now that is not open to professional athletes. But many Olympic boxers become professionals after the Games. One of these was Muhammad Ali. Many people say that he was the greatest boxer ever. He said this himself – *often*. He was the most famous too. But when he won a boxing gold medal in the 1960 Olympics, he was known by a different name, Cassius Clay.

Clay proudly returned to his home town of Louisville, Kentucky. He wore his medal all the time; he even slept with it. But the early 1960s were a difficult time in the south of the United States. One day, Clay tried to go into a local restaurant. He was refused because the restaurant was for 'whites only'. There was a fight with some of the restaurant's customers. Clay angrily threw his gold medal into the Ohio River. Not long after he was named the best professional boxer in the world, Clay became a Muslim. He took a new name – Muhammad Ali. Some people have questioned Ali's story about his Olympic medal. But at the 1996 Olympic Games in Atlanta, Ali was given a new gold medal.

Olympic Greats — Teófilo Stevenson

One of the best Olympic boxers of all time never became professional. His name was Teófilo Stevenson, and he was from the small island of Cuba. He won Olympic gold medals in 1972, 1976 and 1980. He was offered five million dollars to fight professionally in the United States. Stevenson said no because he wanted to stay in Cuba.

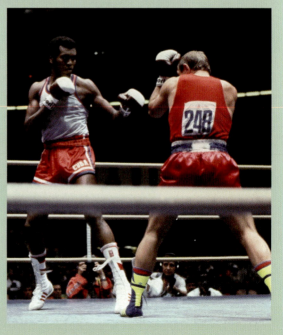

CHAPTER 10

In the Hands of the Judges

Of course, nobody could get a 'perfect 10'. That was impossible! But then Romanian
Nadia Comăneci – only fourteen at the time – started to compete.

In many Olympic events, it is easy to see the winner – the first athlete to the finish line, the team with the highest score. But in some sports, it is more difficult. Judges must watch the athletes and give them points.

In the Pool

In the diving events, judges watch and choose the best athlete. The most famous Olympic diver is the American Greg Louganis. He competed in the 1976 Games in Montreal at the age of sixteen. He did not win a medal there, but eight years later in Los Angeles Louganis won the gold medal easily.

In Seoul in 1988, Louganis was winning in the early part of the competition. But then he made a terrible mistake. He started a dive badly and hit his head. When he hit the water, blood was coming from his head. Was Louganis out of the competition? No, after twenty-five minutes, he was ready for his next dive. He was only taken to hospital after he won a place in the final part of the competition. He won a gold medal the next day.

A week later, Louganis was diving for a second gold medal, against a great young Chinese diver, 14-year-old Xiong Ni. It was a close competition until Louganis's last dive. It was not an easy dive – or a safe one. Some people called it the 'Dive of Death'! But Louganis succeeded and won the gold medal.

In the Gymnastics Area

There have been gymnastics competitions for men since the first modern Olympics in 1896. A women's team event was introduced in 1928; from 1956, women started to compete alone. Both sexes do the floor exercise events; the other events are different. Gymnasts can win medals for each different event; there is also a medal for the gymnast with the best total score.

Gymnastics was very important in Eastern Europe after World War II. The Soviet Union produced a lot of gold medallists. Between 1956 and 1964, the female gymnast Larissa Latynina won eighteen medals – nine of them gold. That is more than any athlete in any sport. But the most famous gymnast from the Soviet Union was a 17-year-old called Olga Korbut. She was only 1.5 metres tall and weighed just 39 kilos. She won three gold medals at Munich in 1972, but not for the best total score. The world did not mind: Korbut's smile became a favourite memory of those Olympics for many people. She was the most famous gymnast in the world. But four years later at Montreal, there was a new star in women's gymnastics.

Olympic Memories – The perfect 10

At the Montreal Games, the judges' scores were shown on an electronic sign. But there was a problem: the highest score on the sign was 9.95 out of a possible 10 points. It did not show 10. Of course, nobody could get a 'perfect 10'. That was impossible. But then the Romanian Nadia Comăneci – only fourteen at the time – started to compete. On two different events, she received 10 points from all seven judges. Unable to show her true score, the electronic sign showed '1.00'!

At the 2008 Olympics, Chinese gymnasts were the most successful in the men's events. There were eight gold medals to win. The Chinese men took all except one.

On the Ice

Some of the most beautiful events at the Olympics are on the ice. In events like ice dance, art has an important part to play. Ice dancers carefully choose their music and even their clothes. Judges do not only make decisions about the athletes' skating skills. They also decide how beautiful or exciting a dance is.

The 2002 Winter Olympics in Salt Lake City showed the dangers of having judges in sport. In one event, the Russian pair Yelena Berezhnaya and Anton Sikharulidze was competing against the Canadian pair Jamie Salé and David Pelletier. The two Russians competed first and received good scores. But the Canadians seemed faster and more exciting on the ice; in the opinion of the North American crowd, their skating was perfect. They started to shout, '6.0! 6.0!', the highest score possible. But five of the nine judges gave the Russian skaters higher scores and people were angry.

The story quickly became a big problem. 'Were some of the judges acting unfairly?' people asked. The Olympic organisers moved quickly to solve the problem. The Russian skaters did not lose their gold medals, but the Canadians received gold too. Years later, people are still unsure what happened. Some think that there *was* a problem with the scoring. Others think that the judges just had different opinions about the very different kinds of skating by the two pairs. But the rules for judges were changed soon after the 2002 Games. Now only nine of the twelve judges' scores are chosen; of these, the highest and lowest scores are not used. The total score is given, but not the scores of each judge.

Olympic Greats – Torvill and Dean

At the 1984 Winter Games in Sarajevo, British skaters Jayne Torvill and Christopher Dean were already the world's most successful ice-dance pair at that time. But at the Olympic Games they did something really special. For their music, they chose *Bolero* by Ravel. This presented them with a problem: the music was four minutes and twenty eight seconds long, but the time for the free dance programme was only four minutes and ten seconds. Dean found an answer in the sport's rule book. The clock only started when the athletes were skating. So for the first eighteen seconds of their dance, the pair moved on the ice on their knees! The clock started when their skates touched the ice.

On the day of the free dance final, the pair arrived very early in the morning to practise in private. But during the dance, the twenty or thirty cleaners there stopped their work and watched. Later that day in the final, the Olympic judges agreed: Torvill and Dean's ice dance was really special. Out of a total of eighteen scores, they received twelve perfect scores of 6.0.

6.1 Were you right?

Look at your answers to Activity 5.4. Then complete the sentences below.

1 If two weightlifters lift exactly the same weight, the .... athlete is the winner.

2 After a nine hour wrestling final in 1912, the judges gave both men a .... medal.

3 Fights between Olympic boxers are shorter than .... fights.

4 Gold-medallist Cassius Clay .... his name when he became a Muslim.

5 The .... in the gymnastics area was not able to show Nadia Comăneci's perfect scores.

6.2 What more did you learn?

Answer the questions.

1 What did Muhammad Ali do with his gold medal?

....

2 Why didn't Teófilo Stevenson fight professionally?

....

3 Why did Naim Süleymanoglu continue to compete?

....

4 Why did Torvill and Dean start their most famous dance on their knees?

....

....

5 Why did blood come from Greg Louganis's head?

....

6 Why did Jamie Salé and David Pelletier receive gold medals?

....

6.3 Language in use

Look at the sentences on the right. Then complete the sentences below with the correct form of the word on the right.

> Lifters **compete** in different weight groups.
>
> Before the **competition**, they are weighed.

1   .... fighters are strong, skilful and fast.   (success)

2   He was offered $5,000,000 to fight ....   (profession)

3   Olympic boxers wear .... on their heads.   (protect)

4   Some people have .... Ali's story about his medal.   (question)

5   Many of the Soviet Union's .... won gold medals.   (gymnastics)

6   Before Nadia Comăneci, people thought that a perfect score was

    ....   (possible)

6.4 What's next?

Chapters 11 and 12 are about the best and worst sides of the Olympics. What do you think these are? Look at the pictures in the chapters and make notes below. Add other ideas.

Best of the Olympics	Worst of the Olympics

CHAPTER 11

The Need to Win

But Lewis was not happy: in his opinion, Johnson won the race too easily. Something was wrong.

Olympic athletes want one thing most of all – to win. To follow this dream, they train and practise for many long, hard hours each day. The cyclist Victoria Pendleton won a gold medal at the Beijing Olympics. The British athlete started in the sport as a young girl. It was not always easy: 'I didn't like it some of the time. Some of the time I hated it.' An ordinary day for her is:

> Morning: Two or three hours of training with weights. As a cyclist, she works most on her lower body.
>
> Afternoon: Three hours on a bicycle. On some days she rides shorter distances against the clock on a bicycle track. On other days she rides out on the road.

This kind of day is not unusual for many athletes. Before competitions, the swimmer Michael Phelps trains for five hours each day, six days every week. He also eats *a lot*. Phelps must eat six times the amount of food that most adult men eat in a day. When he is not training, rest is very important. 'Eat, sleep and swim. That's all I do,' Phelps told a reporter.

Against the Rules

For a few athletes, the need to win is too strong. They decide to break the rules. At the Montreal Olympics in 1976, Boris Onyshchenko of the Soviet Union was near the end of a long, successful time in the pentathlon. On the second day of the team competition, he was fencing against an athlete from the British team. In Olympic fencing, a light goes on when one athlete scores a hit against the other. But there seemed to be a problem. At times the light came on when Onyshchenko was not very near his competitor. This happened against other British competitors too. Finally, the organisers checked Onyshchenko's equipment and found secret electric equipment there. To score a hit in the competition, Onyshchenko only had to press something with his hand.

Drugs at the Games

Drugs are a big problem in modern sports. Athletes want to win, and drugs can make them faster or stronger. It can be hard for some athletes to say no. Athletes were first tested for drugs at the 1968 Olympics in Mexico City.

In the twenty years after the 1968 Games, forty-two athletes failed their tests. But people believe that many more competitors took drugs. Sometimes governments *gave* the drugs to their athletes. In 1977, Olympic runner Renate Neufeld ran away from East Germany to the West. She explained how sports training worked in her old country. Her trainer told her to take a drug. Neufeld did this at first. She stopped when she started to grow a moustache! When she refused to continue her use of the drug, the secret police questioned her about her refusal. Soon after this, Neufeld decided to leave East Germany. In the world of East German sports at that time, she said, her story was not unusual.

Olympic Memories – A long wait

In the 1968 Games, British boxer Chris Finnegan won a gold medal. After the fight, he had to take a drugs test. But there was a problem. He did not need to go to the toilet! The scientists waited and waited. Finally, at 1.40 in the morning, Finnegan succeeded. He passed the test.

● Too fast to be true

The most famous case of drug use in the Olympics is the Canadian 100 and 200 metres runner Ben Johnson. At the 1988 Games in Seoul, Johnson broke his own world record in the 100 metres race – he ran the distance in 9.79 seconds. At the finish line he held one hand up in the air: the sign meant 'Number One'. The American Carl Lewis – the gold medallist from 1984 – was second. But Lewis was not happy. In his opinion, Johnson won the race too easily. Something was wrong.

Ben Johnson's happiness at his Olympic win in 1988 did not last long.

Lewis was shown to be right. When Johnson took his drugs test after the race, the scientists found a drug. The gold medal in one of the Games' most important events was taken away from Johnson. The story shook the world of sport. Later, Johnson tried to tell young athletes not to make the same mistakes. 'It happened to me,' he said in tears. 'I've been there.' But not all athletes listened. In 2010, thirty athletes could not compete at the Vancouver Winter Olympics because of their results in drugs tests before the competition.

The organisers say that the discovery of drug use by athletes is getting more and more difficult. In Beijing in 2008, 4,500 drugs tests were given during the Olympics. The organisers of the London 2012 Olympics made plans to test half the competitors.

A Change of Country

At the age of seventeen, in 1983, the South African runner Zola Budd held a world record at 5,000 metres. She wanted to run – and win – at the Olympics. But no South African athletes could compete in international sports at that time. Budd's grandfather was British, so she moved to Britain. At the 1984 Olympics, she ran in the 3,000 metres race for her new country.

Many people were already unhappy about this. Then, during the race, as the athletes fought for the best position, the US favourite, Mary Decker, hit Budd's legs from behind. Decker fell to the track in pain. Her Olympic dream ended. Budd too failed to win anything.

After the race, Budd went to Decker. 'I'm sorry, I'm sorry,' she said.

'I don't want to talk to you,' replied Decker.

Race organisers studied the video later. In their opinion, Budd did not act wrongly during the race. But the crowd on the day – and Mary Decker for years after that – thought differently.

Budd looks back at Decker in the women's 5,000 metres race in 1984.

CHAPTER 12

Olympic Dreams and Memories

He was the only runner on the track and the pain was clear on his face. Many of the crowd returned to their seats and shouted for the brave Tanzanian.

Pierre de Coubertin's dream of the modern Olympics has been alive for over one hundred years. Of course, in that time there have been problems, but there have also been wonderful examples of Coubertin's hopes for the Games.

Brave Losers

Every athlete wants to win a medal, but sometimes the other athletes in an event have shown the best side of the Olympic Games.

● John Akhwari

In the 1968 Games in Mexico City, marathon runner John Akhwari was one of only three athletes from Tanzania. He started the race well, but after about 29 kilometres, the race became harder and harder for him. He was so tired that he fell. He hurt his leg and was in pain. But Akhwari did not stop. He was in last place now, but slowly he ran to the stadium.

A lot of people were leaving because the race was already won. But then Akhwari came into the stadium, more than one hour after the race winner. He was the only runner on the track and the pain was clear on his face. Many people returned to their seats and shouted for the brave Tanzanian. As he crossed the finish line in last place, Akhwari became a part of Olympic history. Later a reporter asked him why he did not stop. The athlete's reply became famous: 'My country did not send me 7,000 miles* to start the race. They sent me 7,000 miles to finish it.'

● Derek Redmond

In Barcelona in 1992, the British runner Derek Redmond recorded the fastest times in the early races of the 400 metres competition. He was hoping for a gold medal. But then, in the race before the final, his Olympic dream died. He was running well, but 175 metres from the finish he fell to his knees. The look of terrible pain on his face told the story. As the other athletes finished, Redmond got to his feet. In great pain, he slowly tried to run the rest of the race. It was too much for Redmond's father. He ran out on to the track and put his arms around his son's shoulders. Organisers tried to stop him, but he waved them away. Father and son crossed the finish line together. Later, Redmond's father said, 'He had to finish. And I was there to help him.'

---

* 7,000 miles: about 11,000 kilometres.

Redmond did not compete as a runner again and in his doctor's opinion, this was the end of his days as a top sportsman. But Redmond had other ideas. He worked hard and won a place on his country's basketball team.

● Robina Muqimyar

When Robina Muqimyar was a child, the government in Afghanistan did not believe in sports for girls. She also studied at home, because there was no school for girls. But after a change of government, it was easier for Muqimyar to train. In 2004, she was one of the first two women ever to compete in the Olympics for Afghanistan. When she ran in the 100 metres race, she covered her hair. She wore long trousers too. In Athens she was seventh in her race; in Beijing four years later, she was last. The results did not matter. After her long fight to be a female athlete in Afghanistan, Muqimyar was a winner in the eyes of the world.

After the Games, she decided to become a politician in her home country. She wanted Afghanistan to be a fairer place for women and children.

Friends around the World

In Coubertin's opinion, the Olympics Games should bring the world together. For many Olympic athletes, this has been true. Competitors often look back happily on their time in the Olympic village with new friends from every corner of the world.

● Friend to friend

The Australian long-distance runner Ron Clarke was a great athlete, but he did not win any Olympic medals. On his way home to Australia in 1966 after a competition in Europe, he stopped to see his good friend Emil Zátopek. The Czech athlete gave a small gift to Clarke. When the runner opened the present back in Australia, he could not believe his eyes. It was Zátopek's gold medal for the 10,000 metres final in 1952.

● Hand in hand

Ethiopia's Derartu Tulu was the first black African woman to win an Olympic medal. She competed in the women's 10,000 metres in Barcelona in 1992. Near the end of the race, there were only two runners at the front: Tulu and a white South African called Elana Meyer. This was the first Games for South Africans in years.

In the race, Tulu was running close behind Meyer. Then, with only 420 metres to the finish line, she passed the South African and won. After the finish, she and Meyer – the first black African gold medallist in a women's event and South Africa's first medallist since 1960 – ran around the track together and waved to the crowds. It was a great example of everything that was good about the Olympic Games.

Tulu and Meyer after the 10,000 metres final in Barcelona

The Closing Ceremony

At the end of each Olympic Games, there is another ceremony – the closing ceremony. It is a time to look back on the high and low points of the Games. But it is a time to look to the future too. The Olympic flag is taken down. Then it is given to someone from the next host city. As the people of the world watch, they look forward to the next Games four years away.

They know that, like the Olympic flame, Pierre de Coubertin's dreams for the Olympic Games will not die.

1 What do you think?

a Look at the statements below and write the numbers 0–5 next to them.
5 means that you completely agree with the sentence. Write 0 if you
completely disagree with the sentence.

1 Coubertin's dreams for the Olympics came true. ☐

2 Athletes should be able to earn money from their sport. ☐

3 Women should compete in all Olympic events. ☐

4 Drug-takers should never compete again. ☐

5 Athletes from rich countries win more because they have better

   equipment and training. ☐

6 The Olympics should be a competition between athletes, not countries. ☐

7 The Olympic organisers should drop some events from the competition. ☐

8 There should be one home for the Olympics, not a different city for

   every competition. ☐

9 Too much money is spent on the Olympics. ☐

b Discuss your answers with another student. Give reasons for the numbers
that you wrote.

2 In your opinion, who were the greatest Olympic athletes of all time? You can choose athletes from this book or other athletes.

a Make a list of five athletes.

b Discuss your list with two other students, giving reasons for the names on your
list. Together, try to agree on a final list of the five best Olympic athletes ever.

Greatest Olympic athletes	
1	4
2	5
3	

1 Choose an Olympic story from this book that you are most interested in. Make notes about it here:

Notes

Year and place:
Story:

2 Use other books or the Internet to find out more about this story. If possible find a picture of it. Write a report here.

Great memories in Olympic history

3 If possible, put all of the reports together on a real class or school website. If not, put them on the classroom wall for everyone to read.

Many organisations give money for sports or use sports to help people. These organisations often need money from people.

1 **Work in four groups. Make notes, then talk about your organisation to the class. Explain why you should receive money. After that, have a class discussion. Which organisation should you give money to?**

Group A   Your organisation takes poor children from city centres to riding schools. Here they can learn to ride horses and to look after them.

Group B   You work for a national organisation that buys sports equipment for disabled athletes. This helps them to train for the Paralympics.

Group C   You are looking for money so that a young local gymnast can stay near the country's best training centre.

Group D   You work for a national organisation that visits schools. Special trainers help young children to try new sports for the first time.

2 **In small groups, find a real sports organisation that helps people through sports. These questions may help you to choose.**

- Do you want to choose a smaller, local group or a national or international organisation?

- Do you want an organisation that is interested in one sport or lots of sports?

- Who do you want the organisation to help?

Report back to the class about the organisation that you have chosen. The class should discuss all of the organisations. Which one will you make money for? The class should decide by a vote.

Plan a 'School Olympics' or 'Classroom Olympics' event to make money for the organisation in Activity 2. Answer these questions with another student. Then discuss your ideas as a class and make decisions.

- When and where will you hold the event?

- Will you need permission from anybody?

- Who will the competition be open to?

- What events will there be? (Think about equipment. Will the events be serious or silly?)

- How will you make money from the competition? (Will competitors pay? How much? Will people pay to watch?)

- Will the winners of each event get anything?

- Who will organise the events? (Who will be judges?)

Make a poster to tell people about your School Olympics. Remember to say where and when the competition will be.

5 On the day of the competition, students should do one or more of the following jobs.

Organisers:
- Decide the order of events.
- Call athletes to the start of each event.
- Record the results and the winners.

Reporters:
- Make notes of what happens in the events.
- Take photos or, if possible, film some events.
- After the competition, write a report about it for a school newspaper or website.

Athletes:
- Try and win your event!

6 When you have the money from the School Olympics, send a cheque to the organisation from Activity 2. Write a letter to put with this. Say why you chose that organisation. Explain what happened on the day. Write the letter in English first, in your notebook.

Dear Sir/Madam
We are students at the Oxford School in Ankara. We decided to hold a 'School Olympics' to get money for your organisation. There were lots of events.